# THE ELIJAH MESSAGE

# THE ELIJAH MESSAGE

## ACKNOWLEDGING GOD'S VITAL PATERNITY

## THE MESSENGER

Blue Dolphin Publishing, Inc.
1993

Published by Blue Dolphin Publishing, Inc.
P. O. Box 1920, Nevada City, California 95959
Orders: 1-800-643-0765

ISBN: 0-931892-76-7

**Library of Congress Cataloging in Publication Data**

Elijah (Biblical prophet : Spirit)
   The Elijah message : acknowledging God's vital
paternity.
     p.   cm.
   ISBN 0-931892-76-7 : $6.95
   1. Spirit writings.  2. Second Advent—Miscellanea.
I.    .  II. Title.
BF1311.E46E46  1994
133.9'3—dc20                  93-21290
                                            CIP

Cover art: "Elijah and the Widow" by Jan Massys (1509-1575).

First printing, November 1993
Printed in the United States of America by
Blue Dolphin Press, Inc., Grass Valley, California

5  4  3  2  1

# ⊷⇒ CONTENTS ⇐⊷

*"Learn of me, for I am meek and lowly in heart."*
—Jesus

# PREFACE

THE ELIJAH MESSAGE, with its various segments fitted together, is a spiritual mosaic picturing God's grand "Design of the Ages," revealing not only what He is presently up to, but also what He has always been about in His dealing with His family of children on the earth—developing them to spiritual maturity in His image and likeness.

God's munificent purpose in creating a spiritual race of humans to inhabit and have dominion over all the earth has been lost. Through the restored truth in this Message, the knowledge and understanding can now be regained even as the next progressive step in His planned ages unfolds—the old and failing Age of Grace now giving way to the millennial Age of Righteousness and the brotherhood of man.

The six millennia of civilization's history allotted for the development of mankind's spiritual first fruits are now coming to an end, together with all the religious and state systems that ruled the lives and hearts of people through questionable principles and inept and inequitable practices. These systems held all of the nations of the world in bondage until the spiritual elect ruling body could be called out and perfected, leading the way for all others to follow.

This Message, with its mission to restore the truth that was lost, sets the stage for the return of Jesus Christ (Acts 3:21, 22) whom heaven was to receive until the time of restitution of all things, and it fulfills Jesus' prophecy in Matthew 17:11: "Elijah truly shall first come and restore all things." It also fulfills completely the end-time prophecy (Malachi 4:5, 6) performed earlier in part by John the Baptist, and this time by the Elijah spirit heralding the second coming of Christ.

Thus, the author of *The Elijah Message* is the spirit of Elijah. The messenger chosen to deliver it was born on a farm in DeKalb County in northern Indiana, March 17, 1918. He was the third child in a family of seven children, born to Protestant parents, and early on was indoctrinated by both parents and his maternal grandparents into the Christian faith. Close to the age of six he had his first contact with the spiritual, in which he was shown that he had two lives: one he knew was associated with the heart, and the other had to do with the outer living in time. He tried hard to convey this to his mother and his older sister. He took them into the kitchen, pointed first to his heart, saying "this," then turned over the pages of the wall calendar with its days, weeks and months, saying "that," and excitedly repeated "this and that." However, they did not understand, and he was too young then to realize the significance of what he was shown.

Later, in September, he began to attend the Protestant parochial school in the area until the fourth grade, when his parents and family moved to southern California in 1927. There he finished the eight years of his parochial schooling, four years of high school and one semester in college. Early in February, 1941, at the age of 22, he was drafted into the U.S. Army. As a staff sergeant, he was medically discharged in late September, 1943, after seven months in army hospitals. He returned home very anxious to leave the area and the church where he was so well known—for he had an overwhelming desire to "find the Lord." He soon moved to a foothill area seventy miles away.

He was independent of the church now and was getting settled in his trailer house next to his parent's home when, on an early morning in February, 1944, he experienced an unexpected and life-changing conversion, one of a great spiritual, dynamic unknown, which had never been seen or felt by him in his twenty-five years of association with the church. The great influx of divine love and inspiration, and the Holy Spirit's anointing power, brought a vision experience in which he was ushered into a rather large, windowless room where, above the wainscoting of a long, uninterrupted wall, three individual sentences were revealed, in large, glowing print that lighted up the room. They read as follows:

"The Spirit of Elijah is upon you, Isa. 11:2."

"I have anointed you to bear witness of Me to the living dead."

"The Lord shall set His hand again the second time to recover the remnant of His people, Isa. 11:11."

The Bible references were puzzling, but he knew that he had been quickened by the anointing Spirit and awakened to the spiritual consciousness of the inner life of his earlier vision. Later illumination revealed that the Isaiah 11:2 reference, which refers to Christ, meant that the Elijah Spirit now had membership in the body of Christ, the true church. The term "living dead" had reference to the potential elect, who were stalled in their spiritual progress and needed assistance in finding the way of deliverance from sin. The Isaiah 11:11 passage referred to the preparation of the spiritual remnant (elect) for their role in the upcoming great tribulation and its interruption by Christ coming in to install righteous rule.

The afterglow of the experience lasted for some months, bringing the realizations that spiritually it equalled the miraculous Red Sea crossing foreshadowed in Exodus 14, that the wilderness path of the heart's regeneration to spiritual perfection under the Holy Spirit's guidance was now before him and must be traveled in order to obtain salvation from sin, and that this could not be done vicariously.

Before 1944 had run its course, a Protestant minister came into his life and brought to his attention the most startling news that he had ever heard: Christ's work of salvation was universal, and all will be saved in God's great Plan of the Ages. He and his parents were overjoyed and carefully studied the numerous scriptures that confirmed, "In Christ shall all be made alive." The minister had come by this knowledge only a few months earlier, through a flash of revelation as he opened the parsonage door. Many in his congregation accepted the teaching, but the church officials did not. A year or so later he was gone, and his successor disavowed the teaching entirely. The absence of the Holy Spirit's presence in the church was then keenly felt by the messenger. It was time for him to look elsewhere.

The messenger, a carpenter by trade, built a few new homes but mostly remodeled older ones and sold them. He made enough money to take off occasionally to travel and investigate various religious faiths and practices throughout California and adjacent states. The Spirit gave him free range to look into and know what was going on but never encouraged him to join anything. In general, Christ's way of salvation through suffering was rarely embraced or followed. Alternate paths to the standard path set by Jesus were everywhere. None of them dealt effectively with the problem of self and sin; the lower nature was not being replaced by the higher. Without the Holy Spirit and the heart's regeneration, the goal—perfection in the image and likeness of God—was not being reached, and the truly righteous conduct of the Christ-life within was very seldom seen.

On vacation one autumn, with addresses in hand of groups devoted to the spiritual wisdom of the East, he looked up a number of them, from southern California to Mount Shasta. Many of the devotees were in their thirties and were very congenial and sincere in their seeking. When told about his quickening and conversion experiences, sometimes a few of the women would cry, as did one middle-aged man who was a group leader. The experiences were just what they sought and longed for but were unable to find. None of them were caught up in false hell-fire and annihilation doctrines and so were generally receptive to the universal salvation teaching that involved God's Plan of the Ages.

He attended many Pentecostal-type meetings and revivals, hoping to find among them some evidence of the Holy Spirit's gentle nurturing presence and the resulting meek and lowly behavior. What he found instead was loud music and shouting, hell-fire-and-brimstone preaching, a confusion of tongues with no interpretation, and wild, emotional demonstrations that in no way reflected the Christ-like spiritual nature.

He tuned in many times to view the televangelists in their heyday. Certainly, there were television ministries that had spiritual integrity, but most of those that were led by "charismatic" personalities—who he watched with dismay, seeing their highly planned programming and advertising expertise, and their endless appeal for funds—reduced their Christian faith to no more than a money-powered religious enterprise, wholly devoid of the Holy Spirit.

Probably the most difficult alternative paths being offered, some finding widespread acceptance, were and still are those devoted to what might be called mental science, involving mind training and the transformation of the mind. According to the Holy Spirit, "These paths fall short; their gain is minimal for the true life in Christ. Many of their membership are out on their own, not as yet rescued; while they do have laurels, they are not spiritual. They can be seen at the bottom of a big cliff—with no guide to show them the way to the top through the regeneration of the heart."

Such teachings put undue emphasis on the mind at the expense of the heart's regeneration. The sinful lower nature, which needs to be displaced by the incorruptible, higher spiritual nature, is motivated by the heart's desires or "feeling springs," and it is to these that the remedy for sin must be applied. It is the heart that utilizes the mind and not the other way around. Thus, the heart, as source, must become the primary focus of attention in the spiritual transformation from self-centered to God-centered consciousness, in order to utilize the "mind of Christ" with its ability to serve God rightly.

"Out of the heart of (unregenerate) man proceed evil thoughts, adulteries, murders, covetousness, pride, etc." Yet all these things that defile humans will, in the regeneration of the heart and under the operation of the Holy Spirit, tend to the good in the end—when we understand that they conduct us toward a greater capacity and appreciation of the good. The fiery purification process develops into the character of man the divine love attributes of God: compassion, mercy, forgiveness, patience, meekness and all the virtues that define and characterize the gentle nature of spiritual people.

In 1976, when his many investigations left him somewhat comfortless, the messenger was given the following information: "You are a bringer of light from the Father, a coordinator, a representative of the Father. You are kept in balance through the Father's power only, not through man's. You are sent to approve or disapprove the elect, lifting them from the human understanding into the spiritual understanding."

These words from the Holy Spirit gave him renewed faith and courage—and the knowledge that the divine commission was still intact, that once again the Father's concern was for the prospective elect to stay the regenerative course until perfection is achieved, and that efforts be made to increase their numbers. But as yet he was unaware that the commission would find fulfillment through a divinely inspired restoration Message. The first indication of that Message came late in 1984, when the Spirit's first promptings began, and an outline of the Message came into focus. Surprisingly, at the same time the gift of spiritual intuition was opened up in his older sister, providing the ability to hear the "still small voice" within and its word-for-word transmission.

Due credit is here given to the sister for her invaluable assistance. Although she did not collaborate in the writing of the Message, she was occasionally given information, augmenting what was coming through him, that the Spirit had him work into the Message. Also, during, and particularly after, the writing, she brought welcome corroboration, some of which is given in the Appendix. She confirmed the completion of the Message as follows:

> "The Message is well-contained, applicable, thoroughly conceived. It is supreme in the eyes of the Lord, as a witness to His testimony in the deliverance of all in the Father's planned ages; a divine accomplishment, dealing with a message of love in the restoration of all in God's image, and ready for distribution."

Now to all readers of the Message who are stranded in their spiritual transition, and to teachers and those in leadership roles, the Holy Spirit would point out to you the standard path taught by Jesus that He for our sakes traversed in order to show us the way whereby we, through identification with Him in His humiliation, suffering and death to the natural, might gain the resurrection, life and glory of His divine, spiritual consciousness. This, also, is the path that is fully confirmed by Paul in his Epistles and is now carefully delineated in the Elijah Message. "For he that hath suffered in the flesh has ceased from sin; that he no longer should live the rest of his time in the flesh to the lusts of men, but to the will of God." (1 Pet. 4:1-2)

Among all the groups that the messenger looked into, he found some who have developed a "knowing" ability from experiences imparted and derived through worldly life. These have become immersed enough in earthly experiences to appreciate the things of the Spirit, because earth's empty vanities have brought into their hearts a longing and yearning for God and the spiritual life. When the outer glamour of the world and the sensual life have lost their appeal, and the soul is ready and eager for spiritual awakening and anointing, and when it is willing to be led by the Holy Spirit within, then the "call" of God the Father will come. "The election stands not of works, but of Him that calleth."

All those who are called will find that the initial quickening by the Holy Spirit—the opening up of spiritual consciousness and life—will be highlighted by a great influx of compassionate love and inspiration that opens up the soul's intuitional faculty and sends them on the journey that will release them from sin and instill the righteousness of Christ within.

There will be oases on the wilderness way of purification—areas of quiet happiness, of needed rest in the "peace that passeth understanding," and even sweet consolations. These, however, are not the goal. For all who are committed to the regenerative path and progressing on it, there will soon come the knowledge that inaction and inactive bliss cannot for long satisfy the soul that is motivated to reach perfection in Christ and find fulfillment. The fulfillment comes through individual usefulness being united in the great universal wholeness and oneness of the purposes of God. And it is this spiritual union that brings the unbounded, everlasting joy and blessedness that so honors and glorifies God, our great creator.

We are in a time of great moment for the Elijah Message to become more widely known in order to do its intended work, that of emancipating and edifying many, and of encouraging individual groups of the newly enlightened through reinstating the truth about God's universal love and purpose of the ages—groups having their lives and understanding released from the chains of ecclesiastical dogma, dominance and power. They will now be free to serve the Lord rightly, directed by the Holy Spirit within, turning many hearts and minds to God for their deliverance from self and sin.

It takes real courage to follow after Christ, who said, "No man can come to me, except the Father which hath sent me, draw him." May the Father now draw you and reveal to you Christ's path of spiritual regeneration, as it is reaffirmed in the Elijah Message, and grant you the faith of Abraham, the "friend of God" and exemplar of undaunted courage. When called out, Abraham willingly put God before all else and obeyed Him, for which God accounted him righteous.

# INTRODUCTION

THE ELIJAH MESSAGE is a Divine accomplishment, dealing with a message of love, in the restoration of all in God's image and likeness. It is an effort to instill a strengthened faith in God the Father's integrity that would allow for a higher love interchange between Him and His family of children on the earth.

This Message sets out to restore the truth that has been obscured throughout much of the Church Age, to shed great light, and to dispel the centuries-long night of spiritual darkness—a night that saw an early departure from faith in the Holy Spirit's anointing, nurturing and transforming power. It brought instead a clinging to the legal, formal, dogmatic spirit of outwardly religious man, which is powerless to save from sin and unable to promote the *vital* divine-spiritual love.

Certain themes in the Message are intentionally repeated, for it is the Father's objective that more about the true spiritual life will become known as the next age emerges and that both the knowledge of the Holy Spirit's inspirations and the soul's awakened spiritual faculties of intuition, perception and discernment will be more widely acknowledged as the manifestation of the first fruits draws near. This is so that the elect may be unfolded, perfected, matured and conformed to the model of Christ Jesus, the archetype; ready to be empowered for their glorious divine usefulness in the establishment of righteous government on the earth.

So, the vital contact with the Holy Spirit is to be emphasized and the efficacy of the Spirit's power confirmed in the development of a spiritual, immortal race of humans. The knowledge of good and evil is instrumental in the trial, education, training and perfecting that are to bring humans to spiritual maturity in God's great Plan of the Ages. The power of the Holy Spirit, imperative in the regeneration of the elect, will be indispensable in the lifting of more and more souls from the lower level bondage to sin into the higher spiritual life, free from sin. For the impending, unprecedented judgments and the overturning of the old order will usher in God's spiritual age and kingdom with an ever-increasing regeneration. And it will be only through a more widespread understanding of the spiritual that the life and reign of Christ will prevail and the meek inherit the earth.

Acquaint yourselves, then, with the inner spirit of Christ, even in this fast-paced, end-time of the Age; engage in earnest searching, prayer and seeking until He is found within. Then the true spiritual values will come out and the eye become more watchful to achieving God's purpose of delivering from sin and sanctifying the soul, making it fit to partake of Christ's kingdom of righteousness. Give all glory to God the Father who, through Christ and the Holy Spirit, creates within man

His image and likeness as perfected sons and daughters of God.

The benevolent Heavenly Father, seeing the end from the beginning, knew that much greater good would come from the experiential knowledge of both good and evil. He realized that the temporary evil would conduct His children to a greater capacity and appreciation of the gracious spiritual life than could otherwise have come.

"The sufferings of this present time are not worthy to be compared with the glory which shall be revealed in us. For the earnest expectation of the creature waiteth for the manifestation of the Sons of God." (Rom. 8:18, 19) These completed sons and daughters of God will effectively introduce the virtuous, spiritual "thought seeds" into the earth, transmitting to more and more the higher-consciousness life, in an ever-increasing regeneration throughout Christ's reign on the earth.

How the greater life and glory are attained through the heart's regeneration and will ultimately include all, is clearly outlined in the Message.

NOTE: Unless otherwise indicated, all quotations are from the authorized King James Bible with, however, corrections made where the Greek was mistranslated.

# THE FATHER'S CONCERN

WITH THE SPIRITUAL SIGHT OPENED, lo, many of the church ministries were seen to be not of God but of the will of man, and the Gospel of the Ages was not being preached. Rather, all were in contending church sects in various presumptions in a sharp departure from the will of the Father. And grave judgments were impending that would shake awake in many the inner consciousness that relates to the mind of Christ and God's spiritual heart of love.

The Message herein given is addressed to all those seeking the kingdom of heaven within, where the serving and inspiring of others and the utter forgetfulness of self is the regular life of everyone. It makes its appeal to those church leaders and followers stalled in their spiritual progress because of false and misleading doctrines embraced by the outer church for many centuries and who, should true doctrine be restored, would seek and find renewal. To all such, even at this late date, an invitation to enter or re-enter the kingdom is here given. And the Message will address itself to the restoration of major portions of truth that, through mistranslation or misinterpretation, have been lost or are no longer rightly apprehended. And it will involve itself ever more deeply in reviving a true concept of God's paternal desire and prerogative and in restoring the primacy of the Holy Spirit in the believer's life.

In every human heart a correspondence with the Divine Parent within waits to happen, and some such special communion with Him does at times take place—a contact with the inner divine-spiritual is made. However, in the great majority thus awakened, the personal relationship with the Lord is not understood, deepened or enlarged. All too often a malfunctioning religion is standing in the way, and the opened-up spiritual intuition, with its ability to follow after Christ, is soon overlooked. The gracious Holy Spirit is shut out by its antithesis—the legal and formal self-righteousness that leaves the heart unregenerate still. Much of the visible church is presently in such a spiritual dearth that it impedes, rather than promotes, the kingdom of heaven within.

So apostate is the nominal church today that it has forged a widespread consensus that the rule of the moral law of the flesh with its sin must be mingled, somehow, with the spirit of life in Christ Jesus in order to insure the salvation of the soul. Nothing could be further from the truth, for it is the Holy Spirit alone that sanctifies, and, with its spiritual love, both supersedes and fulfills the moral law. The church's misguided attempt at blending the lower nature with the higher spiritual has resulted in the *lukewarm* internal condition that is most distasteful to God and inimical to renewal. The fallen nature under moral law and the spiritual life under divine love are mutually exclusive. Until this is understood, the church's ability to facilitate the calling out and perfecting of the elect will be seriously impaired, and it will continue to grow the spurious believer—the natural, moral elite that, in the Message, are referred to as the living dead—those who are yet without a consciousness of God and without the overcoming spiritual life within.

Many professing believers are without the spiritual contact, and the Father and the Son are not being revealed to them through the informing Holy Spirit within. The neglected intuitional faculty of the soul in man is still unable to receive the Spirit's vital inspirations and know his good tidings of salvation from sin.

# THE LIVING DEAD

IT IS THE SPECIAL PURPOSE of the Message to bear witness of God to the living dead, best described as carnal believers—those who seek to know God, have had some spiritual work begun in them, but who are not following through. They are would-be Christians whom God earnestly seeks but who are perplexed and disenchanted because of the incongruities in the orthodox teachings regarding the way of salvation. They remain in the lower, Adamic nature and live under its influence and power. Some of them certainly could be reclaimed, their numbers augmenting the end-time True Church, for whom a second outpouring will soon be in order. God's Plan of the Ages moves on methodically, and his purpose according to the election "stands not of works but of Him that calleth." This, then, is His call to all the faltering believers—to become vitalized afresh and to continue their spiritual journey to the end.

Many sincere souls are unacquainted with the way of the heart's regeneration, with its death to the lower, sinful nature and the arising of the new spiritual life with its overcoming power. They are unaware of the personal work of the Holy Spirit within. The "old man of sin" cannot fall into the ground and die and the new creation spring up, grow and mature without the Spirit's power.

Christ's precepts, "Love your enemies . . . do good to them that hate you; pray for them which despitefully use you," (Matt. 5:44) and Paul, on agape love, "Charity (love) suffereth long and is kind . . . envieth not, vaunteth not itself" (1 Cor. 13:4)—these are a divine spiritual constitution that must be honored but cannot be by the natural, self-willed man who is without the spiritual life. The intellect of man cannot commune with the risen Christ, cannot absorb His supernal selfless life. For that, the intuitional faculty of the soul is vital. It is quickened at conversion and maintained through continual, heartfelt desire for the Lord.

Conversion's new birth is a temple of the Holy Spirit living within. Saving faith is more than just a knowing about God and a belief in Bible history. It is, rather, an intimate relationship with God through the Holy Spirit. It is because of the intuitional contact that the Holy Scriptures become the Living Word, that the nurturing and reliable guidance from within becomes possible and that righteous conduct flows. It is because of an overall lack of such Holy-Spirit life in the nominal churches today that the carnal membership—the living dead—are not being developed spiritually, are not being lifted above the claims of self and used only in the helping and serving of others. And it is why so many of the young in the professing church are turning to the flesh in a vain attempt to find the fulfillment that can come only from the Spirit.

The carnal believers need to be rescued from blind dependence on dominant personalities and ecclesiastical powers, from outer pomp and display, to an awareness of and greater confidence in the guidance coming from the Holy Spirit within. Prayer and earnest seeking will open up the intuitional perception to receive the Spirit's inspirations more widely and directly, allowing many seekers to actually know God, learn to discern His will and receive His saving grace with its righteous flows.

It should always have been the primary work of evangelists, pastors and teachers to bring sinners to the point of conviction where they resolutely turn to the nurturing of the Holy Spirit within and remain faithful to Him until Christ is formed in them. It is imperative that the believers have an indication, an intuitional knowledge, of what is going on inwardly if they are ever to be freed from the lower bondage to sin and, through the spiritual love, be brought into the glorious liberty of the children of God.

# THE HOLY SPIRIT'S WORK

WHEN CHRIST WAS ON THE EARTH, He very ably revealed that the help that comes from the Lord is from the life and action of the Father's Spirit within. When the prospective believer comes into a realization of this, the desire to experience the inner spiritual can be roused. When, then, the quickening from the Holy Spirit comes, the divine image-seed, deep within, is awakened or stirred into activity, and the first contact with the environment of God—the spiritual love—is made. From this, the saving faith takes hold in the believer and keeps him or her in the newly-found atmosphere of love. The spiritual consciousness is born, and growth begins and continues as the bonding with the Holy Spirit holds and the confidence in Him increases.

The new birth experience evokes in the sinner repentance; the guilt is removed and the sins forgiven. The way of salvation from the lower to the higher consciousness, then, is open. The way is a process of regeneration with its trial and testing—"being made perfect through suffering." Truth comes into play throughout the entire transit of the course. It is not a static but a whole series of revelations and inspirations that promote the spiritual life and growth, that separate the soul from self-hood and sin, and that instill the righteousness of Christ within. Humility becomes known as the key spiritual requisite. As long as the self-will is subject to the will of the Father and the believer stands humbly in His field, the spirit of truth continues to afford the spiritual lifeblood of Christ in the Word until maturity is reached. In the recovery of the soul, the Holy Spirit's nurturing and directing power is indispensable.

It is the commission of the true church to preach the Gospel and to acquaint everyone with the way of regeneration as the evolving soul becomes ready for the awakening and capable of being led by the Holy Spirit within. The visible church has always found this concentration on the inner life difficult to do, particularly the encouraging of the aspirant to pursue the purification process to the end. Rather, an apostate church itself becomes the way, allowing the spirit of truth to be supplanted by the doctrines, symbols and ceremonies of the church. The aspirant is expected to find nourishment and guidance in these rather than from the life and inspiration of the Holy Spirit.

If the hapless believer finds contentment in the church's control, outer learning and thinking for him, his spiritual consciousness will fail, and the lower personal love and goodness will seem to suffice. These will be mistaken for Christ's righteousness and will be substituted for the higher, selfless love. Such will remain nominal believers, living dead, in whom the world is still predominant; for, without contact and submission to the Holy Spirit within, the power to overcome the world, the flesh and the devil is simply not in man, and the righteous conduct does not flow.

From the many and large religious organizations down through the entire Church Age, it was always only a remnant that came under the aegis of the Holy Spirit and were brought through by Him to spiritual perfection. "Be ye therefore perfect, even as your Father which is in Heaven is perfect," (Matt. 5:48) is a divine directive asking for a complete submission to the will of the Father. Only this leads "Unto a perfect man, unto the measure of the stature of the fullness of Christ," (Eph. 4:13) where the higher spiritual consciousness prevails and the divine conduct finds outlet in mature sons and daughters of God, no longer in a selfhood, apart from Him—who have "put on the New Man, created in righteousness and true holiness."

# THE PLAN OF
# THE AGES

WHEN THE LONG-NEGLECTED TRUTH about God's Plan of the Ages is restored, when all the mistranslations and misconceptions that rob it of its glorious purpose are removed, and it becomes fully known, it will elicit joy and thanksgiving to God the Father for His infinite love and wisdom and to Christ, "by whom also He made the ages." God's eonian purpose and grace were given in Christ "before the foundation of the world" and "before the times of the ages began." The plan involves the work of successive stages or orders, in a continuous act of creation, during which God deals with humankind through a series of eons or ages by different methods—developing His children from Eden's state of innocence to the spiritual maturity befitting a son or daughter of God, but "every man in his own order."

It is the purpose of the ages that all of humankind involved with sin be rescued from the bondage of its corruption and be raised into the glorious "liberty of the Sons of God." Humanity, as God well knew, would fail the test in Eden and thus be exposed to the lower estate by God, who has a very specific and beneficent end in view. "All things are of God." "He doeth according to His will in the army of heaven and among the inhabitants of earth: and none can stay His hand." (Dan. 4:35) Accordingly, it must be that all things are worked into His plan and that they further His gracious purpose.

In the first chapter of Genesis and the first three verses of the second chapter, the *prophetic* account of creation is given as it *will* be in the perfect, finished result: man in the image and likeness of God. It is spoken of by God as if it were already done. "Declaring the end from the beginning, the things that are not yet done, saying, my counsel shall stand." (Isaiah 46:10) "Even God, who quickeneth the dead, and calleth those things which be not as though they were." (Romans 4:17) And it is seen by God as being "very good." The *historical* account of creation begins, then, in the remainder of the second chapter of Genesis, and it sets forth the process by which the creation of the divine race of man is to be accomplished, *i.e.*, through a descent by way of generation into the soul's self-conscious state of natural man. In a journey out and away from conscious unity with the Father, able to relate to both good and evil, humans—strong in self-will and with freedom of choice—were, through trial and error, to gain knowledge through many and varied experiences. Predisposed to sin, humans, in self-love and without due regard for God and for others, would involve themselves in evil until, at length, satiation or saturation would set in and turn them back to the Father. Christ, then, as humanity's spiritual savior, would, through the inner awakening, repentance and regeneration involving the work of the Holy Spirit, bring humankind to spiritual maturity and a greatly enhanced appreciation of God.

Some former ages, such as the Patriarchal Age and the Age of the Law, were meant to develop in man an active conscience through the contact with good and evil, a keen moral sense of the depravity of the fallen nature, and the absolute necessity for the spiritual recovery. Thus, the law, given to hold the lower nature in check, was also to be a child-leader unto Christ and the righteousness which is by faith. In the New Testament, then, it became possible for Christ to open up the Age of Grace and begin to call out from the lower consciousness the first-fruits body of which He is the head, the promised seed. Through Him the rest of humankind are to be blessed and recovered in ever-increasing numbers—multitudes from the Great Tribulation, the large millennial harvest, and, at last, the innumerable hosts coming out from the lake of fire purification. God's grace broadens as the various ages unfold their mysteries—from law to grace, and the finished, perfected elect are brought to all the fruitfulness of the millennial age. Then, "in the dispensation of the fullness of times,"—the last of the ordered ages which condition human life on the earth—"all things will be gathered together in Christ." (Eph. 1:10)

# EON (AGE) MISTRANSLATED

**T**HERE SEEMS TO BE LITTLE REALIZATION by the church that the called-out elect are to reach the intuitional level of spiritual development. Many seem unaware of the personal work of the Holy Spirit in the interpretation of the Scriptures. Only the Spirit's revelation can be perfectly trustworthy and distinct. Its light comes when the soul, touched by the spirit of truth from within, begins the process of change from the natural to the spiritual life. Thus, the change is essential if the Holy Spirit is to make the Word personally viable—it is the Spirit that gives it life. The heavy reliance solely on the intellect of man has led to the many unfortunate disagreements in Bible teaching.

The Greek language was very suitable for the New Testament's divine revelation. All of God's various dealings with man were seen to be age-related (eonial) and the entire Plan of the Ages, no more than the scaffolding in the process of building, creating spiritual man. All this was to change with the coming of the earliest Latin fathers soon after the death of Paul. With their darkened religious psychology, they advanced the mistaken theories upon which the various Christian creeds are based, substantially altering the entire character of Christ's lofty spiritual teachings. Not understanding the inner work of the Holy Spirit, they soon paved the way in countless discrepancies for what was ultimately to become contending church sects. Without the loving Spirit of Christ to unify and guide, the legal and authoritative bent of mind so influenced all of European Christianity that it deflected and declined into many systems of dogmatic hierarchy and centuries of spiritual despotism.

Eonian, the Greek adjective for the word "age," was, by the earliest Latin fathers, made to express "eternal." This gave credence to the base and degrading, everlasting hell-fire and annihilation doctrines that so distort the purpose of the ages and denigrate both the Father and the Son. These doctrines confuse and discourage the prospective believers, who are asked to face a God who is at once the very definition of love and an implacable tyrant—an impossible contradiction! Great harm has resulted from confusing the ages with eternity. The incorrectly-rendered Greek and Hebrew terms "for ever and ever," "eternal" and "everlasting," never refer to endlessness but to a series of terminal periods known as age-times.

The Hebrew word *olam* in the Old Testament, and the Greek word *aion* in the New, both mean age. The entire Biblical conception of the ages has suffered because of their faulty translation. In the New Testament, the transliterated noun "eon" (age) and its adjective "eonian" (age-related, age-during) occur numerous times, and both are repeatedly misinterpreted. The fact that the same word translated "forever," "everlasting" and "eternal," is also translated "world" and "ages," should long ago have galvanized Bible scholars into restoring a true perception of what the Bible actually teaches concerning the ages and the creation of spiritual man. That time is man's journey into the earth and that God made the dispensations and fitted them out for the accomplishing of His "Plan of the Ages" (Eph. 3:11 Rotherham) is now virtually unknown.

For, what was and is yet the purpose of such temporal ages with their evil, but that the good of man might be derived thereby. Their purpose will end when the making alive of the race in Christ becomes as coextensive as its death in Adam. Both the separation from the Father and the return are eonial (age-related). It is only when the ages have run their course and unfolded their mysteries, and the Father has accepted, in its perfect, finished result, the Kingdom from the Son, that "eternal" will become an actuality for the race of men.

# METANOIA
# MISTRANSLATED AS
# REPENTANCE

FORESHADOWED IN TYPE in the Old Testament and alluded to in the New, was the process of metanoia, the spiritual journey from Egypt to the promised land. It was announced for the first time almost two thousand years ago by the herald, John the Baptist, in Judea. It restores the spiritual consciousness and wholeness, without which man is always found wanting, and it is the perfect antidote for the superstition, fear and paranoia of the unrecovered world. It brings rest to the soul. It enables man to overcome the flesh by the power of the Spirit—the flesh being nothing less than the corruptible human nature. Metanoia embraces the entire concept of quickening, repentance and regeneration. It brings man to the spiritual consciousness—inspired, reoriented and overjoyed in the life of the Spirit of Christ Jesus.

Metanoia is a Greek word meaning "change of mind" and also "to have another mind," *i.e.*, the mind of Christ. John the Baptist, bearing witness to a great new light and power about to appear in Christ Jesus, called to the multitudes on the desert, "metanoeite." He had in mind more than just the "repentance" of the authorized version of the Bible. Rather, he envisioned a being created anew, as the "another mind" implied, for, the "Kingdom of Heaven is at hand." Metanoia was also the first word and call given by Jesus on the advent of His ministry. The real concern was the opening up of the spiritual consciousness and the taking away of sin: "That ye put on the New Man which, after God, is created in righteousness and true holiness." (Eph.4:24) Metanoia, thus, brought the inner purity and radiance with its image and likeness of God.

All this was to change when metanoia was mistranslated as simply repentance, beginning with the early Latin versions of the Bible, followed by the fourth century Vulgate and, ultimately, by the King James translation in 1611. Once again that mysterious legal and formal iniquity, always antipathetic to the free Spirit of Christ, was clearly in evidence in this unfortunate mistranslation. It has denied too much of Christianity— the all-encompassing grandeur of the Gospel, which takes in the whole of life and calls upon man to enlarge his consciousness to that of the intuitional and spiritual, and the call that all conduct flow from the Holy Spirit within rather than from a law without—to this very day.

This mistranslation has had the effect of putting undue emphasis on the initial and necessary repentance at the expense of regeneration. Christ, in his great love, sacrificial death and blood shed on the cross, did indeed take the guilt and pay the penalty for all sins. Upon repentance, the sinner is forgiven, but many a prospective believer is arrested in his spiritual developmental at this point, not realizing that the all-important quickening by the Holy Spirit is also opening up the way of regeneration so that the sinful lower nature might be dealt with. The believer does not realize that, in the midst of all the compassionate love, he is being set upon the redemptive course. The great love is the environment of God. From it the saving faith is born, and the spiritual intuition is opened, through which, inspirationally, the Holy Spirit can direct the purification process from within and develop the child of God.

Only the Holy Spirit, by revealing to the believer, personally and directly, the divine will of the Father, can have any real value in effecting the sinner's transformation. The believer who yields his will passively and perfectly to God's will advance rapidly. Other than that, man's self-will continues to be his ruler, sits in the body temple and prevents him from seeing or knowing God, until God's purging finally effects a turning to the Holy Spirit for the complete victory over self.

# ALL ARE
# GOD'S CHILDREN

IT IS SO EASY FOR NATURAL MAN to overlook the fact that he, born of woman after the flesh, is in reality the spiritual offspring of God the Father. However much lowly man would interject himself into God's affairs, it is the divine Father alone who can lay claim to man's soul and be responsible for its development in all of His children. Although it may seem most unlikely at times, nonetheless, all of Adam's seed are held by God in His image and likeness and have an individual usefulness that will ultimately bring them unbounded happiness, that will honor and glorify God their maker.

Humankind, coming from the Father into the world through generation, is unconscious of its spiritual lineage and heritage, and its outcome can indeed look bleak until it is quickened by the Holy Spirit. Then the realization comes that "we have had fathers after our flesh which corrected us, and we gave them reverence: shall we not much rather be in subjection to the Father of spirits and live? For they for a few days chastened us after their own pleasure; but He for our profit, that we might be partakers of His holiness." (Heb. 12:9, 10)

Thus, the awakened, penitent elect submit to the Father's will and the regeneration by the Holy Spirit, aware that the carnal condition, with its separation from God, was temporary. The deity of the carnal condition is the free self-will, to whom unregenerate man submits in order to gain life's experiences, to learn to evaluate right from wrong, and to know vanity and evil sufficiently to feel satiation and turn to the Father for deliverance through Christ and the Holy Spirit.

Challenges constantly arise in the earth life, and daily all must apply themselves to outward considerations, experience the feeling states of others, and be reminded of their position and difficulty; for troubles and cares are equally distributed among believers and unbelievers, and we all profit by them according to our state of development. Nothing is amiss, as it all works together for spiritual good—some to lower their state of degeneration to reach bottom and start their way back to the Father, and others to continue their path of regeneration toward perfection as sons and daughters of God. Both the diverging children and those returning are precious in God's sight; He holds them in the completed Divine image while they await the saving grace which is the gift of God.

The metamorphosis from the natural to the spiritual is dependent on the believer's faith in the power of God. For it is altogether His work that effects the change and not man's, "lest any man should boast." The Father creates the wholeness in us through the Holy Spirit by taking us out of the lower darkness, preparing us as children of the Light. It is through the Father's chastening, the fiery trials and testing that our eyes turn from the earthly and temporal things and begin to see the Lord, begin to sense His infinite greatness. The Holy Spirit brings us to the place where God's eternal purpose of the ages can be revealed to us.

For all those who have gone through the rather painful ordeal of deliverance, it is in the gratitude, humility and stability of being delivered from sin, that the real ones in Christ, the chosen few, become a strong defense for the multitudes to follow and be brought through by the Holy Spirit to spiritual maturity.

Oh, wonderful day of awakening and starting our way back to the Father, finding Him with open arms as we reach perfection in Him—all the necessary circumstances are acquired by the guidance of the Holy Spirit for our transformation to Christ's life and nature, with the ability to serve God in meekness, with love in our hearts for our Heavenly Father and all humankind.

# HELL-FIRE
# AND ANNIHILATION

WHEN THE DIVINE CHARACTER of the Heavenly Father is debased, damage is sure to be done, and faith in His integrity needs to be restored. All of us will humbly admit that the retribution of sin will have to continue as long as the soul continues to live in wanton, bad behavior, and we can accept the disciplinary actions of a merciful Father when their purpose is altogether remedial. However, all that is noble in the heart of man, all that is decent in him, cannot but detest the teaching of hell-fire's disproportionate vengeance and heartless cruelty. We cannot but reject God's being presented to us in a guise entirely alien from the whole tenor of His revelations.

Oh, darkened heart of man that could for so long and so tenaciously cling to doctrines that depict an all-loving Father in the wholesale eradication of His children, or as subjecting them to the sustained torture of a literal, never-ending fire. That the internal burnings of hell or the lake of fire, involving the soul or spirit of man, would involve instead the physical body in material fire, is a gross misconception. All the divine fires or burnings are purifactory and are designed to turn humankind from self-will to the will of the Father, developing in humans the mind of Christ and His righteousness. What other purpose could an unfailing God of love, unchangeable in His nature, possibly have?

Forcing the literal translation of scriptural passages that are obviously metaphorical and snatching others here and there, without due regard for their true meaning and perspective, has led to an unfortunate willingness on the part of many professing believers to attribute to the Heavenly Father an intensity and permanence of cruel wrath that cannot be imagined even in the basest of men. Oh, carnal believers, turn to and remain on the regenerative path until you find within yourselves the divine-spiritual sensibility that perceives the warm, loving and understanding heart of God. From that level of awareness, the enormity and repugnance of the false and degrading eternal hell-fire-and-annihilation doctrines become strikingly apparent—they become unthinkable!

The church's unquestioned acceptance of such abhorrent doctrine reveals its spiritual darkness and alienation from God. Not only are unbelievers put off by such a teaching, but the newly-converted can be seriously retarded as the views they hold of God react upon them. Conditioned by their churches into thinking of God as unforgiving and cruel, it would no longer bother them to become ruthless also—and their devotion to the loving, merciful Holy Spirit within, seriously impaired. Monstrous behavior, ascribed to the Heavenly Father who sent His Son, is most demeaning to God's character with humans and fatal in its results upon their actions and character, and presents a most diabolical example for carnal humans to follow or emulate.

Get down, oh man, into humility, and surrender every false concept and will of your own in your desire to know God as He really is. His jealousy and anger are the emotions of perfect love, to be expected of any devoted parent concerned with the discipline and training of His children. As regards God's purpose in the method used, all revelation points to the perfect man.

Shouldn't we rather, then, see in the Son's high principles and gracious nature, the image, the true reflection and demonstration of God's spiritual love, so that "we all, with open face beholding as in a glass the glory of the Lord, are changed into the same image from glory to glory, even as by the Spirit of the Lord." (2 Cor. 3:18) "Love never faileth." It is the true reality that obliterates self and sin as it advances the race of man.

# SECOND DEATH—
# LAKE OF FIRE

THE PERFECTING OF HUMANITY is essentially done on the earth. Conditions that would promote spiritual progress elsewhere are not set forth in the Holy Scriptures. Rather, the attention is focused entirely on the earthly activity, for we are told that two resurrections, separated by the millennium (Rev. 20:5), will bring everyone back: "They that have done good unto the resurrection of Life; and they that have done evil unto the resurrection of judgment [not damnation]." (John 5: 28, 29) The former, whose names are written in the Book of Life, will, through voluntary regeneration, have passed through death to the fallen nature and are saved. All of the latter, resurrected after the thousand years are finished, will have to conclude their spiritual creation by suffering the second death by way of the lake of fire. Its torment and testing (Rev. 20:10) are not for ever and ever, but "the ages of the ages"—the same term used to indicate the length of Christ's reign. As there is a conclusion to the Son's reign, there is then also a conclusion to the operations of the lake of fire, the second death and its conquering action.

Thus may we see that God's justice and mercy will combine to save man from sin: "According to the working whereby He is able to subdue all things unto Himself." (Phil. 3:21) "He will have compassion upon us; He will subdue our iniquities." (Mic. 7:19) "Fire shall try every man's work of what sort it is. If any man's work shall be burned, he shall suffer loss: but he himself shall be saved; yet so as by fire." (1 Cor. 3:13, 15) In the lake of fire all sin will indeed be banished and the evil work ended, but solely in the interest of the soul's salvation.

Two deaths are required to successfully carry out the Plan of the Ages. The first death is death to the Eden state with its spiritual innocence—by way of generation into the lower kingdom of natural man: "To be carnally minded is death." (Rom. 8:6) And the second death is death to the lower, sinful nature through the heart's regeneration: "They that are Christ's have crucified the flesh with the affections and lusts." (Gal. 5:24) The second death comes as a result of a fiery judgment, and, whether it be endured early and voluntarily, "baptized with the Holy Spirit and with fire," or is induced later through the subduing action of the lake of fire, it is always salutary in that, through fire purification, it creates the spiritual man. In God's heart are found neither malice nor unforgiveness, only justice and mercy. "God is the savior of all men—specially of those that believe." (1 Tim. 4:10) This shows that the voluntary believer's early salvation is special, in that it promotes and guarantees the salvation of all.

Only as the result of the second death, the lake of fire rescue, can the many scriptures that promise a universal Christ with overall salvation be fulfilled. There is a valid reason why Christ's reign on the earth and the lake of fire run and end concurrently, and why relevance to God's planned ages cannot be ignored. This last solemn judgment with its few or many stripes meted out, its death at last to the lower nature in all, brings an end to the enmity. It destroys the selfhood in man with its sin, bringing an end to all death conditions, and it fulfills two of the Bible's most important scriptures: "For as in Adam all die, even so in Christ shall all be made alive," and "He must reign, till he hath put all enemies under his feet, the last enemy to be destroyed is death." Then, the ages having accomplished their purpose, will end, "And when all things shall be subdued unto Him, then shall the Son also himself be subject unto Him that put all things under him, that God may be All-in-All." (1 Cor. 15:22, 25, 26, 28) When the Father at last reveals Himself to all through fiery judgment, there will be a complete willingness on the part of humankind to revere God, our maker.

# THE SALVATION OUTCOME

CHRIST HAS BEEN CENTRAL to the entire Plan of the Ages. "I, if I be lifted up," He said, "will draw all men unto me." (John 12:32) "Therefore as by the offense of one, judgment came upon all men to condemnation; even so by the righteousness of one, the free gift came unto all men unto justification of life." (Rom. 5:18) "Wherefore God hath highly exalted Him and given Him a name which is above every name, that at the name of Jesus every knee should bow, of things in heaven and things in earth and things under the earth and that every tongue should confess that Jesus Christ is Lord, to the glory of God the Father." (Phil. 2:9-11) This scripture reveals an overall purpose, so all-inclusive in its scope, so breath-taking in its vision of the outcome of spiritual love, that it cannot but be that all who have ever lived will one day know reconciliation and, through the Christ-life established within, will enter into the glory of God.

Jesus gave us the remarkable story of the prodigal son. In this simple and touching narrative, God's method of raising His children from infancy to spiritual maturity is clearly set forth, and the strongest evidence is given that the Heavenly Father never loses His tender love for His children but eagerly awaits their return. The story gives the reason to believe that everyone (for all have sinned) will sooner or later find himself in the hopeless pigsty condition and, knowing satiation, will "come to himself." No matter how heinous or besetting the sin, "he wasted his substance in riotous living," the desire for the return journey home will be brought about, and the way of repentance and regeneration will be opened up by the Holy Spirit, and the reconciled believer will be guided back into the arms of the waiting Father. The self-centered prodigal, lost in his self-will, will now find himself God-centered and, through the grace of Christ, fully matured and dedicated to serving the Father's house.

The long-neglected doctrine of the salvation of all could well become the litmus test in identifying the true believer and distinguishing him from the false. Radiations of joy would emanate from the former upon the realization of God's true greatness and glory in his Plan of the Ages. The latter, however, could be roused to great protestations and anger, for he finds his security in religious creeds and a surface righteousness. Without the intuitional wisdom and love established in the heart, the carnal believer can, without compunction, consign myriads of souls to either annihilation or an endless burning in the fires of hell. But the spiritual commandments implanted in the true believer's heart—love to God and love to neighbor—would be so compelling that he could not disregard anyone at all. The two spiritual loves would have to impart their spiritual delights because divine love is inherently a yearning to share everything it has with everyone and because it wills everyone's happiness. That this love exists in the heart of the elect, is because they are open to the Father's love and will, "Who will have all men to be saved and to come unto the knowledge of the truth." Believers know well what "manner of Spirit" they are of, "For the son of man is not come to destroy men's lives but to save them." (Luke 9:56)

Neither the Father nor the Son can be frustrated in their full salvation efforts. To have faith in Him is what the Father of spiritual beings expects of His children. Rather than automatons, He wanted to be in association and in communion with competent and mature offspring, with the capacity to absorb and appreciate His high spiritual life and nature. It was to develop just such an enlightened spiritual creation that the Plan of the Ages was instituted and the contact with the knowledge of good and evil allowed. As we trust Him we become friends.

# THE TRUE BELIEVER

WHAT SETS APART THE BELIEVER, submitted to regeneration, is ever the harmlessness, the meek and lowly nature, with its poise. He is so obviously in love. God has become his environment: "In Him he lives and moves and has his being." He is in a state of peace because he is in a state of love. As he becomes more free of the old self, he involves himself more and more in Christ's righteousness and integrity, and he desires to serve God, which is to serve others. He goes out and about selflessly, bringing evidence of the goodness of divine love. His "pray without ceasing" is his spiritual concentration and consecration. His eye is single—God has become altogether his aim and affection. He is aware that the divine love is of the spiritual lifeblood that gives reality to the higher living and that all hope lies in the awakened intuition and spiritual awareness.

The believer realizes that the great faith he now has was born of the revealed-to-him, divine love and that there is real value and reward in sacrificing his self-will and self-life to the will of the Father. For in the Father's will lie both the pattern and purpose for which he was created. He also knows that without the newly-found intimacy and communion with the Spirit, his former faith was no more than credulity and that, although the scriptures are indeed the word of God, they only took on real meaning when they were spoken directly to his spiritual perception by the Holy Spirit; then they became the Living Word. He finds the Spirit never harsh or demanding but patient and understanding as He keeps His eye on the believer's growth. The Spirit brings about the Christ image and likeness, while displacing the lower imposter who would indulge self and sin while acting as the servant of God without the spirit of God.

Throughout the return journey (the wilderness period of preparation), the pressures and suffering needed for the believer's growth will always be provided. As the wellsprings of evil, the motivations of the self-centered heart, are opened up to view and the sins exposed, the fire of the Holy Spirit burns them away, cleansing out the old human of sin and replacing it with the new. All the sins of omission, resultant from a lack of sensitivity, empathy and concern as they surface, and the sharp distress they bring, work to develop these qualities into the divine heart. Annoyances, antagonism and persecution coming from without and Satan's trials and testing will have to be borne until all vestiges of self are removed. However, faith in Christ, the mediator and advocate, will see the believer through and strengthen him. Christ's gentle spirit-presence and comforting words will often bring sweet consolation.

When the mind dwells on the Holy Spirit there can come a passive contemplation and receptivity that opens to the inner spiritual presence. The "still small voice" finds it possible to speak whenever it gets the attention of the conscious mind. The mental inspirations can be perceived and understood—seemingly heard through the newly-opened intuitional faculty of the soul. The inner presence of the Master is the key to all the love, wisdom and power. He can cast out all fear and, in the midst of the persecution, can alleviate the pain and even bring rejoicing! "Blessed are ye, when men shall revile you and persecute you and say all manner of evil against you falsely, for My sake. Rejoice and be exceeding glad: for great is your reward in heaven." (Matt. 5:11-12)

Thus, at last is developed the spiritual, inner beauty that is flawless, and it is flawless because it is selfless. The believer goes from generation to regeneration, implanted with Christ's seed of righteousness and growing into His likeness, into a perfected child of God.

# THE PASSING AGE

FROM THE VANTAGE POINT of the higher vision, all activity on the earth is seen as spiritual. The Church Age of Grace is now coming to an end and the Kingdom Age of the Brotherhood of Man is about to begin. An overall look at the spiritual ramifications of the age that is passing could be of help. Throughout the centuries-long Church Age we see the race of man continuing to move out and away from an awareness of the Father and, through the orthodox religious systems, gaining needed experiences in the school of good and evil, with the focus on the spiritual, devoid of the Holy Spirit. When the early Christian Church, not long after the death of Paul, devolved into the Romish church, there came the first widespread apostasy with its *outward* religious pursuit, impeding the Spirit's vital work *within*.

European Christianity, compromised with the political and the material, throughout the age depicted the consummate spiritual evil. Indeed, it became so separative and lethal, so out of touch with the divine-spiritual love, that it kept all of the nations of Europe in continual turmoil and contention. Its profound spiritual darkness, cleverly hidden in a legal, formal and moral cloak of false light, ever deceived the masses. Christ's life and light were never in the outward, nominal church; His supernal meekness, compassion, tender love and mercy were not in evidence. There was nothing of the unitive life and harmony of the Kingdom of Heaven; rather there was the subjugation and tyranny that mark the spirit of anti-Christ. Yet, in the midst of it all, God's beleaguered elect were called out and perfected.

When the Reformation brought in some significant light and reform, it soon brought in its train many diverse, contentious denominations that departed from the Holy Spirit and declined into the same legal and autocratic mentality and spirit found in their mother church. They resorted to similar crusades, persecutions and martyrdom of the elect. Because of the greater reach of the numerous sects and the many pressures coming from them, more and more of the elect were chosen out and perfected. That comparatively small band, linked with the new order rather than the old, would pass on the living truth with its strength, would explain the age and bring future change. The Church Age, with its apostasy and spiritual bondage, presented the most compelling evidence that without the Holy Spirit, the lower nature wasn't being overcome and superseded by the divine love.

In this end-time of the age, the visible church, particularly in America, is so apostate as to be in great public favor and willing to make a reach for political influence and power. The church has not elicited the intense pressure and antagonism that the true believer so often enlists against himself from the forces of darkness. It is the Bible's Laodicea, spiritually "wretched, poor, blind and naked," in a serious lack of intuitional life and spiritual love. The large membership is unwilling to sacrifice the self-will and self-life that entering into the Christ-life would entail and that would arouse the enmity and hatred from the opposition. Jesus, in His wisdom, knew this opposition brings the closer contact with the Holy Spirit who alone can insure the believer's completion to spiritual perfection.

Today's widespread fall from grace into apostasy is due not to a departure from an outward profession of Christian creeds, doctrines and traditions, but rather to a departure from the faith in the Holy Spirit's power to break up the unregenerate heart and fashion or create anew the regenerate heart of true love. Spiritual dearth throughout the orthodox establishment signals the critical deterioration that will terminate the old church order through judgment and usher in the harmonious Kingdom Age.

# THE UNEXAMPLED TRANSITION

A S THE SPIRITUAL, economic and social conditions of the world worsen, the need for the entire race of man to find salvation becomes increasingly apparent. The general selfishness has become so prevalent that it has erected strongholds everywhere. All the systems that rule the lives and hearts of men are too much based on self and are in a fatal spiritual decline. They cannot much longer allow humans in self-will to live together in sufficient peace and harmony.

The failures that have always characterized the age that is closing are, in this end-time, being carried into awful intensity, giving us a showcase view of unbridled iniquity and seething contention, together with a proliferation of nuclear arms for total destruction, without the spiritual standing to control them. This cannot but bring men's souls to satiation, with universal strife being the rule and competition the basis of existence, and with excessive power and glory accruing to the aggressive among us.

The complacent apostate church, with its membership numbering in the many millions, is proving no bulwark at all against the rising evil tide. Many would take recourse to more law instead of the liberating-from-sin, higher spiritual life which should be their forte. The church's lack of all-inclusive, selfless love is everywhere apparent and has allowed the spectacular scientific and technological advances to outstrip the spiritual and subjective to such an extent that adjustment through the divine judgment will have to be made. God will have to exercise the power of His great wrath to forestall the dangerous selfishness and moral disintegration that now so threaten the overall spiritual progression. With inexpressible mercy to the incoming generations now at risk, remedial action will be taken to humble and bring down the wanton greed, pride and prejudice that are so distressing and so inimical to social unity.

With materialism and sensualism running to extremes, with alarming drug addition and sexual impurity rivaling the abominations of old Sodom, the American people are courting a "time of trouble." However, as given in Ezekiel 16:49 (RSV), the prophet sees the city's problems as being essentially spiritual: "This was the guilt of Sodom: she had pride, surfeit of food and prosperous ease, but did not aid the poor and needy." This, then, is the ultimate declension, for disregard for the poor, as every cleric knows, is disregard for the Maker, and ruin is the inevitable consequence.

The electronic media, the nation's largest newspapers and the national magazines continue to point up America's serious problems with her minorities and their lack of opportunity and the problems with her hungry, sick and homeless. The national indifference in the face of such glaring inequity and misery reveals a tragic lack of spiritual oneness and a dangerous heedlessness of the duties men owe to each other. This should give pause to all levels of government and to the unresponsive churches, that such a replication of Sodom's *dire* moral and spiritual condition, just prior to her heavy judgment, could involve our nation in severe disciplinary judgment and desolation as well.

The Message, then, is meant to restore the truth about God's infinite grace and boundless love, to win from His children their filial devotion and thus "turn the heart of the fathers to the children and the heart of the children to their fathers," (Mal. 4:5-6) obviating a destructive curse. Whatever amount of great tribulation may be required, it will be mitigated by the knowledge that it was ordered by true benevolence and has as its purpose a breach with the past and the release of new and unsuspected forces in a preparation for the higher consciousness state of spiritual man.

# GOD'S VITAL JUDGMENTS

R IGHTEOUS, DIVINE JUDGMENT will close this present evil age with affliction so grave that its days will be shortened and the Messiah will come in, lest no flesh be saved. Yet its chastening will bring many to salvation; for tribulation's purpose is ever to yield "the peaceable fruit of righteousness." "We must, through much tribulation, enter into the Kingdom of God." The pain and distress get deep within, softening the heart, making it pliable for a higher use, taking it from ignorance and a non-faithful demonstration of love into a communion with the heart of God. The Holy Spirit then fashions it into the divine image and likeness. Paul, knowing this to be the propitious end, would even have us "glory" and "be joyful" in tribulations.

In all of times past, whenever the Almighty exercised His great Wrath, it was directed "against all the ungodliness and unrighteousness of men" who, with hardened heart, treasured up unto themselves indignation and wrath, tribulation and anguish and the righteous judgment of God. But whatever the amount and extent of the holocaust, destruction and desolation permitted at times in the past, the Heavenly Father never acted in opposition to His mercy. Always, He could see through to the munificent end where reconciliation and rehabilitation would be effected for all in future ages. For all of His actions in dealing with fallen humans are not everlasting but simply age-related.

The lake of fire judgment is the ultimate tribulation—a most stringent purification action, a pooling of the fires of trial, testing and internal torment—purifying acts meant to administer justice and purge souls, gauged upon the time it takes to cleanse of sins. Some are given few stripes, some many, depending on the willingness to sin. There is no sin too great for forgiveness, for salvation is by grace and "that not of yourselves: it is the gift of God." (Eph. 2:8)

God's ability to subdue iniquity through purging is truly great, but it is used only to correct and make whole in order to restore the soul. The elect are called out early, not because they are better than others, but because God foreknew that their submissive, child-like faith would make their early purification through judgment possible. "For judgment must begin at the house of God," and if they "scarcely be saved," where else than in the lake of fire could the ungodly appear in order to effect the change from willfulness and wickedness to reconciliation and godliness? Christ's transforming lifeblood, with its ability to serve God rightly, will at last reclaim the most hardened rebels. To teach that the wicked will come up for judgment and chastisement, only then to be annihilated or left writhing in neverending fire, is preposterous and darkens the heart of all who hold such a view. The Bible teaches clearly: "But

where sin abounded, Grace did much more abound."
(Rom. 5:20)

All self-conscious souls coming into the earth,
deep within, earnestly await their deliverance from sin
and evil, and the necessary purging will be provided for
all. In the final restoration through the second death
(that to the lower nature), it will be clearly seen that,
throughout all the ages and to his great glory, God was
always the wise, loving, all-powerful Father, utilizing
His paternal prerogative. He saw the knowledge of
good and evil as essential to the knowledge and experience of the highest forms of good, and to the perception and appreciation of His high spiritual life and
nature. He knew that only through the great contrasts
could lasting joy become fully known and that, from
the physical and spiritual bondage, there would come
the glorious liberty of the sons and daughters of God
with the capacity to receive and rightly wield the spiritual love.

# THE RECOVERY OF
# THE REMNANT

IT IS ALSO A SPECIAL PURPOSE of the Message to attend to the recovery of the elect or remnant, to remove them from their more or less silent and closeted existence among the large nominal church membership, and to bring them out and into a greater visibility. Its purpose includes manifesting more widely and openly Christ's high spiritual precepts and harmless nature, from which the apostate-Christian systems, in their resistance to the Holy Spirit, have departed.

As many of the remnant reach spiritual maturity, and as their gentle presence and selfless service become more in evidence, many souls, because of their example, particularly when the impending fierce judgments fall, will turn to the Holy Spirit within. Their inner spiritual perception will be opened to begin the communion with the Holy Spirit that will lead on to their re-generation to maturity. The lifting of the race into higher spiritual consciousness is dependent, then, on first lifting the elect, the first fruits from the lower understanding into the spiritual understanding, making humankind aware of the purpose of the fall into flesh generation with its good and evil, in order to advance all into an even more blessed state than that of the innocence in Eden.

On those rare occasions when the Heavenly Father intervenes in the overall affairs of man, it invariably denotes the deterioration of the old and dying order, its overturning, and the preparation for a new order or dispensation. Before this, however, the Father makes His intentions known with prophetic inspiration through those chosen to represent Him and through whom He now gives due warning. God always has a faithful spiritual remnant intact that He can resort to in difficult times, who can hear Him and respond to His prophetic voice, who can handle the restoration of truth and the introduction of new light and spiritual endeavor.

Thus, it becomes important that the elect body step forward and become known; for when the order of life is to be changed on a grand scale, nothing so benefits humanity as the manifestation of the first fruits. Through confidence in the elect's behavior, the oncoming, larger harvest is charged and changed. The elect are those in whom the higher order has already been reached through the inner spiritual way and is clearly in evidence in their outward physical life. Thus, by the elect's example, others are drawn over, slowly at first. Then more and more find the inner way and outwardly promote and recommend the divine life until it catches on sufficiently to become generally known and accepted, making possible the Isa. 11 harmony that will establish the brotherhood of man.

Christ is the great architect who came in to follow out the blueprint of the ages in building-creating spiritual humanity. He came in well-equipped, with an inherent ability to draw upon the Spirit of God the Father. Then there are the first fruits, predestined for their special work, their sanctification wrought by the Holy Spirit's power, with their willingness to follow and obey His guidance. He prepares them with the life-blood of Christ, which was shed for all to receive, by following Christ's blueprint and going through regeneration as He did to show us the way. For He was "made to be sin for us," although He knew no sin. He, the "captain of our salvation," was "made perfect through suffering." So must we suffer, as he did, through trying times and allegations, unfounded and untrue, to perfect us. We are His chosen companions, charmed by His goodness and mercy to follow through with Him. We partake of His spiritual life force, afforded by the Holy Spirit, that brought Him such glorious resurrection and that brings us renewal and all the wonder and glory of the unitive life in the Father's house.

# THE ELIJAH MISSION

THE PURPOSE OF the Elijah Mission, with its restoration Message from the Heavenly Father, is to bring in great light, and dissolve the long night of spiritual darkness that was the Church Age. Its purpose, in the spirit and power of Elijah, is to expose the entrenched falsehoods that continue to forestall regeneration and threaten the calling out and advancement of the elect. The Message reveals that God the Father is intent on having His elect ruling body enlarged and intact for Christ's soon coming in Glory. He wants them to be in the humility that exuberates the spiritual and attains the new high calling, that creates peace and love in their hearts toward God and their fellow-beings. Many of them have already been falsely accused, made mockery of and shunned—the feeling states that the chosen remnant always go through for divine mastery, as they are perfected into meekness and humbleness, the false pride no longer having a part in them, as the self in them becomes dead.

The elect are the spiritual age nucleus to be manifested as the "sons of God," for whom the whole creation waits with such "earnest expectation." They are spiritually the "body of Christ;" He is the Head, they the members. So the Isaiah 11:2 passage, which applies to Christ, must be extended to include them. They with Him are a body of "wisdom and understanding, counsel and might, knowledge and reverential trust in the Lord." Their special gift is discernment. They will not judge after the manner of carnal man; for their understanding has been quickened to distinguish between the *dead* in the self-will and the *living* in the will of the Father. They are the beginning of an ever-increasing harvest of souls and are the pattern and pledge that the lower nature, with its sin and death, can be transcended by the higher spiritual life and illumination.

Brotherhood is a state of consciousness and can only be fully realized from the intuitional and spiritual level. To achieve it is to transcend the limitations of the natural man. The impending, unprecedented transition is meant to advance the entire race of humankind. No nation will escape the universal testing, for the changes taking place are for the advancement of humanity as a whole. Many, because of the great tribulation, will reach the saturation stage that will bring them to repentance, rebirth and submission to the love and will of the Father for their regeneration. Ordinary individuals will be seen to have the right kind of knowledge coming from the Holy Spirit within, and brotherhood at the intuitional level will begin to emerge and in due time will be achieved in all the outward physical life as well. It will be harmony that will characterize the millennial reign of Christ. With the devil and the power of his evil influence restrained, it will be an age of comparative rest.

It is thus that the Elijah Message with its mission would prepare the way for the second coming of Christ, who with His resurrected saints and His living, translated elect, will rule the world in righteousness; together they will further a much more extensive regeneration.

Follow the Holy Spirit's inner promptings now and choose Christ and our Father's will for your way of redemption from all sin and evil, so that you might reign with Christ. It is only through a sacrifice on your part, the burning out of the lower self and nature, that the resurgence to the higher, with its resurrection, life and glory, becomes possible. The unprepared will have to await the second resurrection, to be cast into the lake of fire for their purification, to come out whole so that God may be All-in-All when the ages have run their course and accomplished their purpose.

# EPILOGUE

THE ELIJAH MESSAGE brings cleansing and refreshing waters for many to receive and carry, making them vessels of the living word and present truth. It reveals Christ as "the true light, which lighteth every man that cometh into the world." (John 1:9) There is no other truth than that derived from the Father's love, and no other life than to know God within and Jesus Christ whom He has sent. We are now being called to repentance, not to obey the law like the pharisees, but from hearts generating love, hearts submerged in the spiritual love of God, He becoming everything and we nothing without Him.

Deep down inside, we all await the anointing by the Holy Spirit to begin our regeneration to the "image of the heavenly" and virginal unity with God, from whom we have departed. The only difference is that in some the awakening begins sooner than in others. But in everyone the Holy Spirit's quickening will one day take charge and develop them to their spiritual identity, and all priorities will belong to God, and all will become adaptable children in His greater purpose for all, "Vessels unto honor, sanctified and meet for the Master's use, and prepared unto every good work." (2 Tim. 2:21)

The Message is a restoring effort to win back the truth that has been lost. False and misleading doctrines, devoid of the divine love, are very involved in today's serious loss of faith and lack of desire for the Holy Spirit. It is God's great Plan of the Ages that, through sin, corruption, chaos and death to the natural, he moves His children on to the holiness, order and glory of the divine-spiritual in Christ. God's principle of using the knowledge of evil for a greater experience and appreciation of the good is fully warranted—only as it applies to all, hence the many "alls" found in the scriptures that relate to the gospel of salvation.

The ages, with their evil and retribution, are never everlasting but temporary only. Eternal hell-fire and annihilation are "doctrines of devils," projections of Satan's insensitivity and tyranny onto the loving Heavenly Father, that can only impact adversely on God's family of children, delaying their development into the divine image and likeness. "God is a spirit;" we, the offspring that issue from Him, are a part of God, whose very essence is the spiritual love which never fails. From the level of the Father's high and holy love, the wholeness and oneness of all of mankind in Him is clearly seen and known. He will be all-in-all.

The vital judgments of God are time related, and they are remedial only, designed to turn man back to God. They are directed against the corruptible flesh, which is at times destroyed, "that the spirit may be saved in the day of the Lord Jesus." (1 Cor. 5:5) Thus, rebellion and a continual downward course can be disrupted, and sinners remanded to God to await future judgment, of which Revelation's lake of fire is the ultimate. The Holy Spirit in the Message reveals these judgments to be purging acts that are altogether restorative. They are a second burning of trial and internal torment, more stringent than the "fiery trials" of the Age of Grace, but necessary to burn out the old "man of sin" in the recalcitrant.

God's judgments do not violate the free will of man, but, ultimately and invariably, they influence the rebel to desire the Lord for deliverance from sin, allowing the righteousness of Christ to be spiritually wrought. "God will have all men to be saved and to come unto the knowledge of the truth." (1 Tim. 2:4)

There are, among the various religious groups and walled denominations, a few of the elect-body of Christ, the first fruits, who are now finishing in preparation for the oncoming large harvest as Christ returns to the earth. Among the many sincere seekers in Christendom, there are, here and there, those who are completed— immersed in the spiritual love and capable of receiving the Holy Spirit's transforming inspirations directly. These few souls today are God's spiritual guarantors, following after Christ to perfection, passing on His Plan of the Ages for all humankind.

In omitting the Holy Spirit's way of transition through the heart's spiritual regeneration, all of the major church systems have been remiss and have left many earnest seekers insensible to the Holy Spirit's operation within, left them unable to consciously imbibe His spiritual life and grow on to maturity in Christ.

Loving God "with all thy heart, and with all thy soul, and with all thy mind and with all thy strength," the first spiritual commandment, from which the second—"love thy neighbor as thyself"—ensues, is impossible without the quickening by the Holy Spirit and a coming into God's environment of divine love. From there the saving faith takes hold and the communion with God begins. And there, beyond the thought system of natural-intellectual man, the Holy Spirit's guidance and teaching from God's word of truth in the Holy Scriptures initiates the transformation from the unregenerate man to the spiritual creation in Christ. All of this is discerned spiritually as we take the time and effort to apply ourselves to the task of hearing the "still small voice" within, in order to live Christ's life without, with its compassionate love and selfless service.

The Elijah Message is meant to increase the present small number of the elect through much more widespread turning to the Holy Spirit's transforming power within, as it restores a true understanding of the Heavenly Father's paternal desire and prerogative in His dealing with His family of children on earth, through His ordered and beneficent grand Plan of the Ages as given in 1 Cor. 15:22-23: "For as in Adam all die, even so in Christ shall all be made alive. But every man in his own order," and by the Holy Spirit of God.

And the Message is meant to prepare the way for the Messiah's imminent return to the earth with kingdom, power and glory. As a very troubled world enters the decade of the 1990s, governmental transitional pressures, which have become evident everywhere, will continue to mount, bringing climactic, grievous and "perilous times," as the inept and inequitable social and economic systems of the temporal superpowers and all the walls of the apostate church systems are brought down to make way for the incoming divine-spiritual economy of Christ the King.

All of the nations will be humbled and any ecumenical uniting of the churches in their present unacceptable condition will be short-lived. For the present world-wide yearning for a truly fair society and a more mature race of humanity will find fulfillment only through the wisdom and power of Christ's spiritual love—in the righteousness and authority of the Son of God's millennial reign as humans become more and more receptive to the unitive Holy Spirit of God and come into an enlightened realization and appreciation of God's vital paternity, of the brotherhood of man, and of Christ the Lord as Savior and King: "The good tidings of great joy, which shall be to all people."

# APPENDIX

## Divine Revelation and Inspiration

Inspired writing, particularly when it is aimed at effecting great change such as during the closing of an age and the transition to another, comes from the Holy Spirit's high vantage point and great power of revelation and the Spirit's infallible guidance in the choice of words from the writer's own vocabulary. This was the method used in the transmission of the Elijah Message through its author-messenger.

Inspired writing can also come from the opened up gift of spiritual intuition in the writer, with the ability to hear the "still small voice" within for its word-for-word transmission. This was the method used in connection with the author's older sister, who is credited in the Preface to the Message for her invaluable assistance and unusual corroboration of the restored and startling truths in the Message.

"At the mouth of two witnesses . . . shall the matter be established."

What follows are excerpts from the sister's writing regarding the Message, its mission, its timing, regeneration, the elect, and the rescue.

## The Message

The Elijah Message is a message of hope, joy, peace and love for all, written by the inspiration of the Holy Spirit, with meekness and humbleness in the heart, giving all honor and glory to God the Father. It is His will that it be spread throughout the world for the sake of righteousness—to lighten the hearts of the people entering into the millennial rest.

The mission of the Message is an organized endeavor, led by the Holy Spirit that confirms the redemption of all and gives advanced knowledge and understanding, with revelations revealed for all, and with true love ignited by the Holy Spirit's power to cleanse and perfect all of God's children—through the doing of His will and the coming into Christ's likeness, everyone in his or her own order, so that God may be All-in-All.

The Elijah Message is a pattern for man to follow, given in condensed, synopsis form, and following the precepts of the Holy Scriptures. It is distinguished through its proper analysis with the correct Biblical translations and interpretations, following God's will and having His approval, in a task of love for the complete restoration of all humankind. For no one can live forever in the behavior of the "natural man." Ultimately, all will live the Christ behavior of the spiritual man.

The revelator has control and manages the wording of the Message in a distinctly unique way, with all glory going to God the Father, which eliminates the margin for human error. Thus the good news will be delivered in all its greatness. In due time, everyone will be blessed by the restored truth—from the greatest to the least—for the accomplishment is complete for all, through the love and sacrifices of our Lord, and the power of His and our Father's Holy Spirit.

## *The Mission*

The Elijah Mission comes in against great odds, but it is substantial and solid. In groups here and there it will attain great favor and high approval with lasting results. In all fairness and honesty, its message reveals the salvation of all and allows hope and optimism to lead the way.

The Message is in for significant review, but words and intellect alone cannot convey its spiritual importance and impact, which the Holy Spirit alone can do. Heavy discussions and arguments will take place; nevertheless, the Message's truth cannot be repudiated. With its dissemination, endorsements will be in the offing, and wise decisions will come after earnestness—all are God's children in His completed Plan of the Ages. This is pertinent, and we labor not in vain toward this goal—that God may be "All-in-All." The more spiritually evolved will see the Message clearly and will help bring along all those who sincerely seek the way back to God the Father.

God always has a faithful remnant, His elect instruments, and these are brought back again to an awareness of Him so that they show to the great multitudes the living evidence of regeneration.

The approaching of the millennial age will now begin to rectify the many errors and wrongs of the passing age. In an ever-increasing degree, more men and women will move on to the universal goal, with their spiritual vision opened. They will give birth to true ideals and have the moral courage and faith to step out and allow the Holy Spirit to make its demonstration, by bringing in a new measure of knowledge and understanding of the spiritual love and power that so often was not in evidence throughout much of the Church Age.

## The Message Timing

The Elijah Message, with its calling of love, gathering up its sweet essence and acclaiming its truth, and given through the inspiration of the Holy Spirit cannot for long be restricted to one here and one there. It is to emerge in time for the soon-coming great tribulation, for the final awakening for many. It is a message of joy and hope for all humankind, and of peace and goodwill between humans and God. God is love and sent His Son to show us the way, that we might know the accomplishments of His Holy Spirit which He promised us—to quicken us and guide us through to perfection as children of God. It will be pronounced good when all is completed in the coming ages, with the reconciliation of all unto life everlasting.

The delivery of the Elijah Message at this time is necessary, for there is a dual war going on in the family—children against parents, both being sidetracked without time for one another, and delinquent in their respective duties and obligations, a situation that must be changed. Thus, "Behold, I will send you Elijah the prophet before the coming of the great and dreadful day of the Lord: and he shall turn the heart of the fathers to the children and the heart of the children to their fathers, lest I come and smite the earth with a curse." (Malachi 4:5, 6)

The Heavenly Father's benevolence, as shown in the Message, will turn many hearts to God and increase the number of the elect coming out to await the coming of the Lord, to live and reign with Him in the new age of righteousness when the devil is cast out to deceive the people no more until the end of the thousand years. Then he shall be loosed for a short time in order to identify the stiff-necked for their intense trials and testing in the lake of fire for their purification—to come out whole.

## Regeneration

A great change is about to take place. The earth is primed for judgment. It is a way of bringing my people closer to Me, for My Spirit shall not always strive with men. Their pride and arrogance shall leave them, and they shall humble themselves, and a spirit of meekness shall come over them, and their hearts shall be purified. Many shall call upon Me in the hour of great tribulation, and I will hear them and bring them out to be saved from sin. It all works for good for those who love the Lord and do His will on the path of righteousness, which prepares them for the peaceful millennial age.

All are welcome to enter in through grace, by the power of the Holy Spirit, which leaves them remarkably well-behaved. Advancement is always sure on the regenerative path. Even though it can be difficult at times, the end result is for good, for suffering provides the tension needed for taking the forward steps with Christ.

The "natural man" in generation, with a dual nature of both good and evil, has gone out and away from the Father to get his experiences on the earth, while those in regeneration are coming back to the Father and are spiritually guided by the Holy Spirit. They are taking off the old "man of sin" and putting on the "new man" in the Christ's likeness unto right-eousness. With true assistance he comes to the River Jordan for cleansing, that his sins might be stripped away and he be made whole. With true repentance he crosses over from the man in generation to come out, through regeneration, spiritually matured in the image and likeness of God.

Thus will some finish in this age with the whole truth and become sons and daughters of God for all to follow in the several ages yet to come, for in Christ shall all be made alive.

## The Elect

To become elect, we are quickened by the Holy Spirit and soon begin to recognize and commune with His indwelling presence. This Holy Spirit access is an ever-present help in time of need. It penetrates from God and opens up the "knowing springs" and guides us properly as needed. Through Christ, it introduces us to the Heavenly Father, working in us both to will and to do of His good pleasure and so further our growth to spiritual maturity. Then we can live and reign with Christ in righteousness, being His witnesses to testify of Him and His way of regeneration: suffering through the purification fires, tempered to withstand harsh treatment and false accusations, being insulated from the wiles of the world, reaching perfection in Christ as completed sons and daughters of God no longer separated from Him, but rather, separated from the world. Formerly guilt-ridden, bogged down in sin and disbelief, without purpose, walking in darkness and error, they are now set free by the Holy Spirit and His power that locks us into His saving grace.

The elect realize that they are only the first fruits of a larger harvest that will ultimately include all so that God may be All-in-All. "The earnest expectation of the creature waiteth for the manifestation of the sons of God." Their mission is ever to serve God by serving others. Having gone through the purifying fires, they will be free of the emotional bondage of intensified "feeling states" that will traumatize many during the great tribulation. In this way they can be most helpful. Their examples of courage and righteous conduct will turn many hearts to God and make of the terrible time of trouble, a time also of significant salvation. When the extreme danger threatens, the days will be shortened by the coming in of the Messiah. The elect rapture to meet Him in the air in order to return with Him and His resurrected saints to reign with Christ in an age of righteousness.

### The Rescue

Thousands who have virginal knowledge now begun in them, have no one to lead them onward on the way of salvation from sin. They have been quickened and left stranded in the wilderness in a sorry state of confusion—without the pure way of truth, which has not been opened up to them by the many misinformed churches that are unacquainted with the way of regeneration. They are unprepared for the spiritual adaptation. Sincere seekers are caught between good and evil, with a desire to escape but with nowhere to go, for the professing churches are today in darkness. The true, illumined church, without earthly form, created by the Holy Spirit, with the meek and lowly Jesus as head, is seemingly nowhere to be found

There is so much material grandeur and display in the modern churches today, and the same pomp and ceremony, ritual and symbolism of the past, that the "outward" remains the primary focus of attention at the expense of the "living" spiritual life and development that should be going on within. The heavy dominance by church hierarchy and authority seriously detracts from the Holy Spirit's inner sanctifying work and His vital transforming power.

There is a "spirit of the law" extant in the churches today, with great emphasis on legal morality that is robbing the gospel of its character of pure grace and ignoring the office of the Holy Spirit. It is the labor of the Spirit alone that can work in man both to will and to do of God's good pleasure. It is only under the operation of grace that sinful man, through the Holy Spirit's nurturing and guidance, comes through to spiritual perfection in Christ—created in God's image and likeness—by faith in His inner work.

Hence the Father's real concern and His bringing in the Elijah Message to restore the truth and come to the rescue of all sincere seekers.